BIZARRE BIRDS

BIZARRE BIRDS

By Doug Wechsler

Photographs by the Author
and VIREO

BOYDS MILLS PRESS

Library of Congress Cataloging-in-Publication Data

Wechsler, Doug.
    Bizarre birds / Doug Wechsler ; photographs by the author and VIREO.
    [48]p. cm.
    Includes index.
    Summary: Text and photographs explore the unique habits of birds from our
    backyards and around the world.
    ISBN 1-56397-760-5 hardcover
    ISBN 1-59078-277-1 paperback
    1. Birds—Juvenile literature. [1. Birds.] I. Visual Resources for
Ornithology (Organization) II. Title.
QL676.2 W435 1999
598-DC21 98-83076   CIP   AC

                    Boyds Mills Press
                    815 Church Street
              Honesdale, Pennsylvania 18431
                    Printed in Hong Kong
                 Designed by Charlotte Staub

    First Boyds Mills Press paperback edition, 2004
              10 9 8 7 6 5 4 3 2 1 pb
               10 9 8 7 6 5 4 3 2 hc

CONTENTS

Off to a Weird Start

Halfway through the age of dinosaurs, a feathered creature hatched from its egg. The creature grew up; it spread its wings, and flew. It shared the sky with **pterodactyls**. The feathered creature lost a feather, which fell into the water and sank into the mucky bottom. Over many thousands of years the muck turned to limestone.

In 1861, 155 million years later, the limestone was cracked open and brought to a German scientist, Hermann von Meyer. He studied the feather and named the creature *Archaeopteryx* (ark ee OP ter icks). *Archaeopteryx* means ancient wing. Soon after this discovery other fossils of the entire creature were found.

Was *Archaeopteryx* the earliest known bird? Or was it a dinosaur on its way to becoming a bird? Scientists cannot agree. Unlike today's birds, it had a mouthful of teeth, a long tail skeleton, and claws on its fingers. Like modern birds, it had feathers, wings, and strong, curved claws on the feet.

Since the time when *Archaeopteryx* got stuck in the muck, thousands of **species** of birds have evolved. This great variety includes birds that fly, such as eagles, and birds that don't, such as penguins. Birds range from tiny hummingbirds, as light as a pencil, to huge ostriches weighing 275 pounds (125 kilograms). Birds live in every habitat on the surface of the earth. Think about that. Have you ever been any place where there are no birds? About 10,000 species of birds now live on earth. That means there are at least 10,000 ways for birds to behave, to feed, or to look. Naturally, some of these are mighty strange.

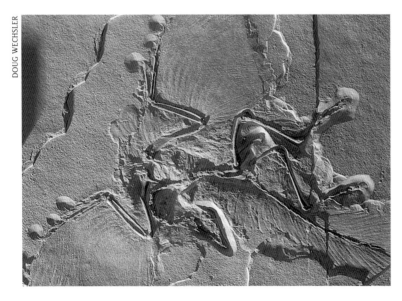

DOUG WECHSLER

Fossil remains of *Archaeopteryx*

Egrets have showy plumes, especially during breeding season.

Chapter ONE

Strange Looks

What Makes a Bird Unique?

There are many things all birds have in common. Wings are one example. However, bats and butterflies also have wings. Scaly legs are another, but lizards and turtles have scaly legs. Birds sing, but the voices of apes and frogs may also be melodious. And it's not the beak that makes a bird unique. A squid has a beak. There is only one obvious feature every bird has but no other creature does—the feather. Feathers make a bird a bird.

Feathers are light and shaped for flight. Feathers provide protection from the heat and cold. They form a shield against biting insects. Flashing bright feathers can send a signal. Mottled brown feathers can hide a bird. Feathers can make a bird look normal or unreal.

Gaudy Feathers

People have long been jealous of gaudy-looking birds. In cultures around the world people decorate themselves with feathers. In the 1800s, it became fashionable for ladies in America and Europe to wear feathers in their hats. Many people made a living shooting birds to sell these feathers to hatmakers. Because of this, several species of egrets and herons almost became extinct a hundred years ago. Showy plumes of egrets were worth their weight in gold. Hawaiian royalty wore brilliant capes made of feathers. Each cape had feathers from hundreds of birds. In New Guinea, bird-of-paradise plumes are still used in elaborate headdresses. In each case feathers make the person stand out. The wearer of feathers impresses (or tries to impress) other people.

Birds use their brilliant plumes for the same reason. Each species finds a way to display its feathers in the best fashion. Male Blue Birds-of-Paradise spread their feathers, call loudly, and may even hang upside down to attract attention to themselves. Why go to all this trouble? Males must be healthy to grow beautiful feathers and perform for hours. The dull-colored female bird-of-paradise watches each male. She studies his feathers. She listens to his squawks. Then she chooses a healthy male to mate with. By choosing a healthy male, it is more likely that her offspring will be healthy too.

Hairless Hairdos

"Featherdos" are often used in courtship. The bushy crest of the male Andean Cock-of-the-Rock covers most of its bill. He cannot fan the feathers out. When courting a female, the male moves in ways that best show off the fancy headgear and bright feathers. This dazzles the female.

The Royal Flycatcher has a very different kind of crest with a built-in surprise. You might say it uses a jack-in-the-box trick. Most of the time the crest is hidden and the flycatcher is a dull brown bird. If it is captured, it fans out its blue-tipped red crest feathers in a semicircle. At the same time, it moves its head from side to side. It also opens its mouth to flash yellow inside. Imagine the surprise to a

Male Andean Cock-of-the-Rock

Royal Flycatcher with
crest fanned out

predator (an animal that eats other animals) that has grabbed it. It may confuse the enemy just long enough for the flycatcher to escape.

The Bald Truth

Only one thing makes a bird look stranger than weird feathers—being bald. We just don't expect birds to be bald. There are good reasons why some birds have bare heads. For instance, vultures put their heads inside the dead animals they eat. Having a bare head is a big advantage for them. Feathers would get messy and hard to clean.

Bald spots can be on other parts of the bird too. Blue Grouse have big, bare eyebrows that change color. Like a stoplight, the change in color sends signals to other grouse. By pumping blood into yellow skin over the eye, the lid becomes red. This may attract females or warn other males, saying, "Move back; stay out of my territory!"

Blue Grouse, with red eyelids

African White-backed Vulture in Kenya

Red-headed Rockfowl in Cameroon

When it comes to bare skin, no bird outdoes the frigatebird (FRIG it bird). Its featherless, red throat pouch is a natural balloon. Beneath the bright red, flexible skin lies an **air sac**. As the frigatebird fills the air sac, the pouch inflates to half the size of the bird.

When it's time for frigatebirds to attract mates, males gather on the nesting ground. They fill their huge chest pouches with air. The brilliant red pouches can be seen from more than a mile (1.6 kilometers) away. When a female flies near, the colony looks like a birthday party with many red balloons. The males raise their wings and chatter loudly. This draws the female down for a closer look.

The reason some birds run around partly naked isn't always obvious. Guinea fowl have mostly bare heads. Does this help keep them cool in the hot African sun? Why does the Red-headed Rockfowl from the African rain forest have a bald red, black, and blue head? And why do many antbirds have bright-colored bare skin around their eyes? Often, we do not know why a bird shows bare skin. Maybe you could become an **ornithologist** (bird scientist) and discover why.

Female frigatebird flies over male.

Turkey Vulture in flight

Chapter TWO

Birds Eat What?

Most of us wouldn't care for worms and caterpillars in our diets. But we are used to the idea of birds eating them. Even the mice that hawks and owls eat seem like normal bird food to us. Why would a bird eat wax, dine on only one kind of snail, or munch on seal droppings? While some birds, such as crows, seem to eat anything, many birds are very fussy about their diets.

Candlelight Dinners

We cannot digest wax, but for a honeyguide, a beeswax candle would make a nice meal. These African birds intentionally lead people and animals such as honey badgers to beehives. The hives are usually in hollow trees. After the honey badger has opened the hive and feasted on honey, the honeyguide settles down to a delicious dinner of wax. We do not know how they digest wax. They either have special bacteria or have special chemicals to break down wax in their guts.

Escargot? (That's French for Snails)

Not all hawks are swift predators able to chase down mice,

Eastern Least Honeyguide
feeding on beeswax

Immature Snail Kite with apple snail

rabbits, and birds. Some hawks feed mostly on slow-moving snails. The Snail Kite, a hawk of the Florida Everglades and South America, is one of these. Its main diet is the apple snail. The kite uses its hooked bill to cut the muscle holding the snail safely in its shell. Young turtles are built somewhat like snails. Kites also eat those occasionally.

Poor Taste

A diet of worms starts to sound good when you think about what vultures eat—**carrion**. Carrion is dead meat. Vultures soar high in the air using their keen eyesight and sense of smell to find dead animals. Few other birds have a good sense of smell. Flying over a dense forest, a vulture can smell an animal soon after it dies. It has to be quick because there is plenty of competition. Once night falls, opossums and other mammals will find the booty.

Sickening Seafood

Snowy Sheathbills live in southern oceans as far south as Antarctica. They are all-white birds with ugly faces. They

Snowy Sheathbill eats dead cormorant.

like to hang out in seal and penguin colonies. What we think is disgusting, they think is delicious. Sheathbills eat dead seals and penguins, seal droppings, and other gross foods. It is good for seals to have this cleanup crew. It makes the colony a healthier place.

Clay, Rocks, and Feathers as Snacks

Macaws, at first view, have it pretty well. They eat a diet of nuts, other types of seeds, and fruit. They also eat clay. In the Amazon rain forest, macaws and other parrots flock by the hundreds to certain riverbanks. They spend hours gnawing away at the clay banks. Minerals in the clay are important to the health of macaws.

Scarlet and Red-and-Green Macaws visit clay bank for minerals

Red-necked Grebe feeding
feather to young

Grebes (GREEBS) don't eat clay, but swallow their own feathers. Grebes are waterbirds that eat fish, crayfish, and insects. Eating feathers is about as nutritious as eating hair. Feathers are tough to digest. The small feathers stay in the grebe's stomach to protect the soft stomach lining from fish bones and other sharp items. Later, the grebe throws up the feathers along with the bones.

Another item on the bird menu that would be tough for us to swallow is grit—small rocks and sand. Grit is great for grinding. Birds that eat grain, such as pheasants, ducks, and turkeys, keep grit in their gizzards. The gizzard is a bird's muscular second stomach that grinds food. The extinct, giant moa, a flightless bird bigger than an ostrich, kept as much as five pounds (2.3 kilograms) of grit in its gizzard.

A Bird Not to Eat

In 1990 an ornithologist made an unusual discovery. John Dumbacher was studying a robin-sized bird in New Guinea. He found out that the Hooded Pitohui (pit a WEE) could kill you—that is, if you ate one. This was the first time scientists knew of a poisonous bird. Fortunately, Dum-

Hooded Pitohui

bacher did not find out the hard way. He licked a small wound on his finger after handling a Hooded Pitohui. Suddenly his tongue felt numb and tingly. Curious, he later tested the feathers and skin in the lab. He found out that these birds have a toxin very much like that of poison dart frogs of South America.

Pitohuis live in New Guinea. Natives there know the birds very well. They hunt and eat most types of birds, but not the Hooded Pitohui. They call the Hooded Pitohui "trash bird." The showy orange and black colors of the Hooded Pitohui serve as warning colors. They warn enemies, "Don't eat me; I'll poison you."

Beak Freaks

You can tell much about a bird's diet by looking at its beak (also known as a bill). Often birds with unusual beaks have strange or specialized diets. The beak is a bird's all-purpose tool. Each kind of beak has a particular purpose. Let's look at some bizarre beaks and how they are used.

The fat, knobby bill of the Reed Parrotbill seems out of

Reed Parrotbill

19

Greater Flamingo in Kenya

place on a small bird. This small songbird dwells in reed marshes on the border between China and Russia. With the hefty bill, it crushes reed stems to get insects living inside the stems.

A flamingo's bill also has an unusual design. When feeding, it is almost upside down. The flamingo is a filter feeder. It sifts tiny plants and animals out of the water or mud. Its tongue acts like a pump. The tongue forces water in and out of its beak. Tiny ridges in the beak trap food particles inside, as water gushes out the sides. The flamingo swallows what is left inside. Did you know that the largest whales feed in a similar way?

One group of ducks, mergansers, has sawlike ridges on the edges of the bills. Their skinny beaks are different from the flat bills of other ducks. Unlike other ducks, mergansers eat mostly fish. This type of beak helps them grab and hold onto slimy, little fish.

Hornbills and toucans are famous for their big beaks. Hornbills live in Africa and Asia; toucans live in Central and South America. Big beaks are great tools. They have many uses. With them, the birds can reach fruit hanging far from

Red-breasted Merganser

PETER DAVEY

Yellow-billed Hornbill
in the Kalahari Desert

their perches. They can dip into deep nests and pull out eggs to eat. If a toucan attacks a poisonous snake, its face keeps a safe distance from the snake. You might think it would be difficult to fly with such a bill, but the bill is very light and hollow.

Long, curved bills make good probes. Curlews and ibises find theirs handy for probing underwater. Ibises reach around sticks or rocks with this fancy tool. Curlews

DOUG WECHSLER

Immature White Ibis probes
beneath underwater rock.

Long-billed Curlew

can probe deeply into mud. Curlews also feed in grasslands. The long, curved beaks probe deeply into tufts of grass. With them, curlews search for beetles and other insects. They can still keep a lookout for predators while eating because they do not have to stick their heads in the grass. Curlews are named for their song, a loud *curr lee*.

Bottomless Pits

Do you eat like a bird? If you did, you would probably not get your homework done. Eating for some birds is an endless task. In the cold of winter a chickadee must eat nearly nonstop. Being small, chickadees lose heat quickly. A belly full of grubs provides the energy that keeps a chickadee warm.

Hummingbirds are the smallest of birds and among the biggest of eaters. A hummingbird may lap up its weight in nectar every day. Nectar is the sugar water that flowers produce. Hummingbirds also eat many tiny insects and spiders for protein.

Flying uses lots of energy and requires lots of food. Many birds migrate hundreds or even thousands of miles nonstop. Fat is their fuel. To get fat, birds go on a feeding frenzy before migratory flights.

A good place to watch a feeding frenzy is Delaware Bay in New Jersey and Delaware. In the middle of May there is enough food on the bay's beaches to fuel millions of birds. Horseshoe crabs supply the bird chow. These strange-looking beasts come by the millions to lay their eggs on the beaches. This happens just at the time sandpipers are migrating from South America to northern Canada. Delaware Bay lies conveniently in between. The sandpipers gorge themselves on the eggs. In two weeks, they double their weight. Now they have enough energy stored to fly another 1,000 miles (1,600 kilometers).

DOUG WECHSLER

Ruddy Turnstone eating horseshoe crab egg

Campbell Island Flightless Teal, one of the rarest ducks in the world

Chapter THREE

To Fly or Not to Fly?

When we think of birds, we think of flight. Birds fly to find food and to escape from becoming someone else's food. They fly to migrate to better breeding areas. Males fly to show their stuff to females. Most birds love to take to the air, but a few are grounded.

Weak Wings

The thousands of islands of the Pacific and Indian oceans were once home to many flightless birds. Being flightless was a good way to save energy. On the islands, the only mammals were bats. Mammals like foxes, rabbits, and deer never made it over the ocean to these islands. So birds did not have to worry about getting eaten by mammals. Nor did they have to compete with them for food. Instead, they could feed on the ground, eating the sorts of food mammals might eat.

Unfortunately, few flightless birds survive today. Many have met the same end as the Dodo. As soon as people arrived to live on the island of Mauritius (more ISH iss), the birds were in big trouble. After millions of years living without mammals, they had no way to protect themselves. Peo-

Dodos went extinct over 300 years ago.

ple with clubs and spears, and animals that came with the people–rats, pigs, dogs–easily killed them. Over the last couple of thousand years, as people settled on the islands of the Indian and Pacific oceans, hundreds of flightless birds have become **extinct**. That is, the species died out completely. Elephant birds, larger than ostriches, many species of rails, and the famous Dodo are all goners.

A few flightless birds still survive on islands. The Takahe (TOCK ah hay) from New Zealand still exists because some have always lived in a mountain wilderness that has never been settled. The Campbell Island Flightless Teal lives on a tiny, isolated island, still free of rats. Can you guess why the Inaccessible Island Rail still survives? The name gives it away. Its island home is so remote that humans rarely visit. Inaccessible Island is in the middle of the southern Atlantic Ocean.

The flightless Kakapo (KAH kah poh) lives only on small islands in New Zealand. This parrot is one of the rarest birds in the world. Only fifty of them still live. The Kakapo is as strange as its name. While most parrots are

Takahe, a flightless bird from New Zealand, grasps food with its foot.

Kakapo—a nocturnal, flightless parrot

very strong fliers, this heavy bird barely leaves the ground. It can only glide a short distance. It is also **nocturnal** (active only at night). Like so many other flightless birds, the Kakapo has suffered from predators brought to its islands by people. Weasels, cats, and rats can walk right into the ground nests to eat the eggs or young.

Like many island birds, the Kakapo has some weird habits. To attract mates, the male hollows out a bowl in the ground on a mountain ridgetop. Then he blows himself up like a balloon and booms up to a thousand times an hour. The bowl acts like the back of a guitar to amplify the love song. The song carries great distances across mountain valleys. Several males boom from nearby bowls, competing for the attention of the females.

This avian boom box has equally odd feeding habits. Unlike other birds, it uses its strong bill to chew leaves, roots, stems, and fruits. Other birds don't chew. They swallow food whole and grind it in their gizzards. Often the Kakapo chews leaves while still attached to the plant. It swallows the juicy parts leaving the used-up bits hanging. Finding dangling leftovers is one good way to tell that these hard-to-see birds are around.

Large flightless birds living on continents have had better luck than island birds in the game of survival. Birds on continents have always had to defend themselves against mammals such as wild cats, dogs, and people. Few mammals would dare attack an ostrich, the largest flightless bird. One kick from the world's largest drumstick could do serious damage to a lion. Like ostriches, cassowaries can fend for themselves. Cassowaries are huge birds that live in rain forests of New Guinea and Australia. A toenail the size of velociraptor's helps them to defend their chicks from native hunters. The nail is five inches (13 cm) long.

Double-wattled Cassowary

Frequent Fliers

While some birds never get off the ground, others never land there. Swifts are the most **aerial** of all birds. They spend nearly all their waking hours in flight. They come down only to sleep and to nest. Some swifts may even sleep on the wing! When they do come down, their **roosts** (sleeping quarters) and nests are usually in hollow trees, caves, buildings, or cliffs. Some nest only behind waterfalls. Swifts even drink and bathe on the wing. When thirsty or in need of a bath, they barely skim the surface of the water, never missing a wingbeat. Swifts are swift fliers. They can fly over 600 miles a day (1,000 kilometers).

White-naped Swifts

30

Broad-billed Hummingbird
laps up nectar while in flight.

Hummingbirds are the busy bees of the bird world. Some are so small, they actually look like large bees. They beat their tiny wings up to 75 times a second. Like bees, they spend their days feeding at flowers. They are the only birds that can fly backward. Unlike a swift, a hummingbird does not spend the whole day in the air. It feeds briefly, zipping from flower to flower to fill its **crop**. The crop is a food storage pouch between the throat and the stomach. After feeding, it rests a few minutes while the nectar in the crop seeps down to the stomach.

Common Murres with egg on cliff

Chapter FOUR

The Business of Breeding

Breeding is serious business. Birds go to extremes to find mates. There is a lot of competition for the best mates. It seems birds will do anything to find the right partner. Once they do, they must create a safe home to incubate eggs and raise the chicks.

Dance for Romance

Some birds do elaborate dances to attract mates. These dances are called "courtship displays." People and birds dance for the same reasons. They want to be noticed, especially by members of the opposite sex. Sharp-tailed Grouse are among the best dancers of the bird world. They spend several hours a day strutting their stuff, stomping and cackling. Purple air sacs in their necks add color to the performances.

When the dancing is done, it comes time to settle down and raise a family. We think of the perfect bird's nest to be a nice cup like a robin's nest. Not so. Each bird has its own taste in nests and each is different.

JOHN CANCALOSI

Sharp-tailed Grouse male
shows his stuff.

T. MCNISH

Adult Great Potoo with chick

Nests for Lazy Birds

What is the simplest nest? No nest at all. For the Common Murre (MER), a nest is merely a single egg placed on a small ledge on a sea cliff. Because the murre's egg is long and skinny at one end, it rolls in circles when pushed so it does not fall off the cliff. A chicken egg on the same ledge might roll in a straight line. If murres had rounded eggs, it might be great for the fish below, but soon there would be no murres.

In Central and South America, a nightbird called a potoo (POH two) lays a single egg on the top of a branch or stump that is slightly hollowed. The female incubates the egg for a month. When it hatches, the baby bird spends its first forty-five days on this tiny platform. The baby potoo sits very still in the open. Since it is colored exactly like the stump it is very hard for predators to see it.

Why bother to build a nest, if you can find an old one? Owls do this. Great Horned Owls often use old Red-tailed Hawk nests. Canada Geese may lay their eggs in an old Osprey nest. Osprey nests usually sit high atop huge tree

Great-horned Owl nesting
in old hawk nest

stumps. When the goose eggs hatch, the parent geese do not bring food. The tiny goslings must leap from the high nest to reach their parents. Goslings are light and soft and usually are not hurt by the long fall. Once on the ground, they follow their parents to good feeding areas.

Other birds just steal. The Piratic Flycatcher of Central and South America is barely bigger than a sparrow. If often steals nests of crow-sized oropendolas (or oh PEN do lahs). Oropendolas are members of the oriole family. Like orioles, they build long, hanging nests. The tiny flycatcher dive-bombs the larger bird until the oropendola gets tired of it and leaves its nest. The flycatcher then settles down to lay eggs in the huge baggy sack up to ten times as long as it is.

What is worse for a bird than having its nest stolen? Having a Brown-headed Cowbird lay eggs in its nest. Instead of building their own nests, cowbirds always lay their eggs in nests of other birds. Often the real mother does not

Piratic Flycatcher in oropendola nest

even notice the strange egg next to hers. The cowbird egg usually hatches first. The mother who owns the nest is called the **host**. She feeds the baby cowbird and treats it as her own offspring. The baby cowbird grows faster than its nestmates. Because the cowbird is larger, it gets more food. Few nestlings of the host bird survive. Since a cowbird does not have to spend energy raising its young, she can use that energy to make more eggs. A female Brown-headed Cowbird lays thirty to forty eggs during the nesting season. That is about five times as many eggs as its host lays.

Brown-headed Cowbirds live over most of Canada, the United States, and Mexico. Before settlers cleared the forests and brought cattle to this continent, cowbirds were found mostly on the wide-open plains. There they often fed near bison, eating insects scared up by shuffling feet of the huge beasts.

Bison are scarce now, but cows have taken the bison's place. Pastures and farm fields where cows live are everywhere. Brown-headed Cowbirds have adapted well to this change. They follow more cows now than bison. They

Cowbird chick with Yellow Warbler chick in nest

have spread over most of North America. The abundant cowbirds cause big problems for the songbirds whose nests they use. Several kinds of songbirds are becoming rarer as this cowbird increases in numbers.

Smallest Nest

The tiniest nests belong, of course, to the tiniest birds. Hummingbirds build their miniature nests on thin twigs, on the tops of leaves, or even on the undersides of leaves. To fasten them onto leaves, they use one of the strongest substances around—spider webs. They steal strands of spider silk from webs in the forest. The nest of a Cuban Bee Hummingbird, the world's smallest bird, is only 3/4 inch (2 cm) across.

Avian Mansions

At the other extreme are birds that build giant nests. Bald Eagles add sticks to their huge nests year after year. One nest in Ohio used for thirty years weighed over two tons. That is the weight of two small cars.

Few birds spend more time building than Hamerkops.

Black-chinned Hummingbirds, sixteen days old

Hamerkop at its giant nest

Hamerkops are African birds related to storks and herons. The name means hammerhead, which describes the shape of the head pretty well. A pair spends up to six weeks building its nest of sticks, mud, and grass. They can use over 8,000 sticks for a single nest. The tireless pair may build four nests a year. The huge nest has a narrow entrance on the bottom to keep big predators out. When the Hamerkop is finished raising its young, the enormous nest does not go to waste. Many other kinds of birds as well as mongooses, honeybees, monitor lizards, and snakes are ready to move in (but not all at once). Not all animals are nice enough to wait. Eagle-Owls may steal the nest when it is only half done. Unlike the owls, sparrows are willing to share. They move into the walls to nest while the Hamerkop is still busy raising its young inside.

A few birds even build apartment houses. The Social Weaver from southwestern Africa builds one of the largest. Over 100 nests may be built together in a giant condominium the size of a small truck (up to 27 feet or 8 meters long.) The nests are built of grass and resemble a giant

Social Weaver nest

Mallee Fowl on its mound nest

haypile in a tree. This weaver lives only in extremely dry climates. Heavy rain would probably cause the nest to fall from the weight of the water. The huge nests take a long time to heat up and cool down. This helps keep nestlings cool in the desert sun and warm on cold desert nights.

One of the strangest types of nests belongs to a group of birds known as moundbuilders. These nests are more like alligator nests than the nests of other birds. They can be as much as 27 feet (5 meters) across. One moundbuilder, the Mallee Fowl, starts by digging a pit. It fills the pit with decaying leaves, twigs, and bark and covers them with a pile of sand. The hen lays her eggs in the sand. The male then covers them. As the dead plants decay below, they warm up the sand. The male spends several hours a day moving sand around to keep the eggs at just the right temperature. When the eggs hatch, the chicks must dig their way to the surface. Once there, they are on their own. The parents do not take care of them. They must take care of themselves for the rest of their lives.

Golden-cheeked Warbler

Weird Habits Can Cause Trouble

An animal that eats only one food, nests in only one kind of tree, or lives in only one type of habitat is called a **specialist**. We have already met several specialists—the wax-eating honeyguide and the snail-eating Snail Kite are examples. Many species have become endangered because of these unique habits.

Golden-cheeked Warblers nest only in woodland of oak and juniper. They live only in central Texas. The warblers are very picky when it comes to nest building. They will not build nests unless they have bark from old junipers to weave in. Housing and industrial developments in central Texas, especially near the city of Austin, have eliminated much of the woodland with old junipers, so this specialist is in trouble.

Palm trunks are the nesting sites for Fernandina's Flicker. This woodpecker lives only on the island of Cuba. It prefers to nest in one kind of palm, the Sabal Palm. When the palm dies, the trunk becomes soft inside. The flicker drills a hole into the stump and hollows out a nest. The dead trunk insulates the nest, keeping it from getting too hot or too cold. The cozy shelter keeps out rain and en-

Fernandina's Flicker at nest hole in palm

emies. Other birds that cannot drill their own nest cavities use the old flicker holes.

Because it is a specialist on Sabal Palm stumps, the woodpecker is endangered. Many palm groves have been cut down to grow crops. People also knock down dead trunks looking for parrot chicks to sell. If they find flicker chicks instead, the parrot poachers may eat them. Meat is scarce in Cuba.

The Red-cockaded (kah CADE ed) Woodpecker is another specialist on the Endangered Species List because of its weird nesting habits. Unlike other woodpeckers, it nests in living trees, not dead limbs or trunks. Not just any living tree will do. This little woodpecker cannot carve out a nest hole in solid wood. It must use an old, live pine tree that is rotten inside. The living pine provides sap to protect the woodpecker's nest from predators. The woodpecker pecks the bark near the nest hole each day. This causes sap to flow. The gummy sap oozes around the nest hole. Snakes that climb trees to eat baby birds can't stand sticky sap. Once sap gets on snake scales, it does not come off. So the snakes stay out of the woodpecker nests.

Old pine trees have become rare. In the southeastern

S. MAKA

Red-cockaded Woodpecker
at sap-covered nest entrance

White-tipped Sicklebill feeding from heliconia flower

United States where Red-cockaded Woodpeckers live, foresters usually cut pines when they are about forty years old. It takes about eighty years for the tree to rot enough inside for the woodpecker to build its nest. So you see why the woodpecker is in a sticky situation. For the Red-cockaded Woodpecker to survive, special areas must be set aside where some trees are allowed to grow old.

Tropical forests are full of specialists. Because of the many life forms, there are many opportunities to specialize. Laughing Falcons eat mostly snakes. Antbirds spend their lives following army ants and eating insects that escape from the ants. White-tipped Sicklebills are hummingbirds that feed mostly at one type of flower—heliconia. None of these birds could survive in the north. There are not enough snakes, army ants, or heliconias there.

Animals that eat only one kind of food often must travel far to find enough of it. Specialists often need big feeding territories. When tropical forests are cut, it is usually the specialists that get in trouble first. They can no longer wander far and wide for their favorite, but rare, food.

What do specialists, beak freaks, and lazy nesters share in common? They are all adapted to fit in with their environment. They rely on their funny looks and odd ways to survive.

EPILOGUE

We can do a lot more to help birds if we study them. Many birds are still in trouble and will need your help. You might leave a dead tree in your backyard. Plant native bushes that provide fruits or attract insects for the birds. You could speak out at a government meeting about ways to protect their habitat. If you do, the birds will return the favor. Just think about those swifts spending all their daylight hours on the wing. You would be saving swifts that swallow insects you might have to swat.

GLOSSARY

Aerial–Spending most of the time in the sky.

Air sacs–Thin, clear, balloonlike sacs inside a bird's body. Air sacs provide more air to breathe during flight. They help keep waterbirds afloat. In some birds, they can be inflated beneath colorful skin to send signals to other birds.

Carrion–Meat of dead, rotting animals.

Crop–A food storage sac between a bird's mouth and stomach.

Extinct–Gone forever. When the last member of a species dies, the species is extinct.

Host–An animal that a parasite takes advantage of. For example, warblers are hosts to cowbirds. Cowbirds fool warblers into raising their young.

Nocturnal–Active at night. Most owls are nocturnal.

Ornithologist–A scientist who studies birds.

Parasite—An animal or plant that lives off of other animals or plants without killing them. Mosquitoes are parasites on us. Cowbirds and cuckoos are parasites on other birds. Though they do not kill the adult birds, they do harm by keeping them from raising their own offspring.

Predators—Animals that eat other animals.

Pterodactyl—A winged reptile that lived during the time of the dinosaurs. The pterodactyl wing had no feathers. A wing extended from each side of the body to the end of a very long fourth finger.

Roosts—Resting perches, especially for sleeping.

Specialist—An animal that eats only one type of food, lives in one kind of habitat, or needs one type of resource to survive.

Species—A single kind of plant or animal. All humans are one species. Blue Jays all belong to one species. In this book names of species are capitalized. Names of groups of species, such as sparrows, are not.

INDEX

Page numbers in **boldface** indicate photograph